Two Seconds of Eternity

An Experience in Another Dimension

I0626417

ISBN: 979-8-9923613-2-2

First Print 2025

Cover art by: Alyssa Skyes.

Proofread by: Meghan McParland

For inquiries, please contact: alyssaskyes@gmail.com

For all who woke up in a body today—
and for those of us who won't stay in one forever.

A short intro from the author:

I was born overflowing with questions—about life, God, the invisible, the human journey, and what on Earth we're all doing here.

As a child raised within strict religious situations, I didn't have the freedom to voice those questions, but they filled my mind constantly. Like many, I was eventually caught in the plain survival of life. Still, I held on to a quiet knowing: that one day, something would help me make sense of these unanswered questions in a way that felt true.

I think most people, religious or not, are spiritual at heart. We're seekers by nature. We wonder about the unseen, about life and death, heaven and hell, pain and love, the state of the world, and why we're here.

Though my writing is drawn primarily to poetry and prose, this book is something different—it is a recounting of an experience that, in a flash, changed everything.

Two Seconds of Eternity is not fiction. It's a deep, philosophical account of a brief yet inter-dimensional experience—an event that cracked open time and revealed something timeless. What unfolded wasn't a vision or a dream. It was a direct encounter with a realm beyond this physical world, rich with presence and meaning.

This is a metaphysical offering drawn from what I was shown—**something I briefly stepped into and what I learned from being there.** It has altered everything for me.

In that space beyond form, I glimpsed the architecture beneath time, form and reality itself. And in the time since, I've worked to translate that experience into words, with simplicity and existential honesty—so it might be pondered and shared.

Through reflection on these layered themes, I explore the nature of opposites and what it means to be alive. Time, duality, form and formlessness, consciousness, emotion, morality, religion, purpose, and love all thread their way through this unfolding and discovery.

This book invites you to reflect on why and how we are here in this life. It also explores how we merge with the unseen—and how the dualities of our world continually interact with us, shaping how we understand ourselves, our purpose, and the world we are all a part of creating.

This is my account of returning with a fragment of eternity, and discovering both bliss and responsibility in the astonishing, fleeting experience of being human.

Contents

Prologue

For as long as I can remember, I've carried the feeling that something essential was missing. Like a puzzle piece I had left out of my human experience. Even as a child and when surrounded by many others, I felt a deep sense of loss or longing. It was an unshakable feeling that I couldn't explain, as though I was failing myself by not remembering something.

Since this has always been a part of me, this searching has shaped much of my life, guiding me through the years to find something elusive, because honestly, I was not sure what I was searching for. I was aching for clarity and answers that I didn't know the proper questions to. It was as if I had to re-discover some forgotten knowledge, something I knew would one day return to me. I often told myself: *"Remember to remember this time."*

The purpose of sharing this story, this **recounting**, is not to convince or sway anyone towards a particular belief, but simply to record the experience as it unfolded and the insights it offered me. These moments stand on their own, whether met with belief or skepticism.

This isn't meant to spark debate about what's 'right' or 'wrong'—I think so much hurt has come in the name of belief. Instead, this is simply a sincere reflection of what I witnessed and felt. I welcome you to receive or interpret it however it resonates for you. My hope is only to awaken a more philosophical and curious lens, rather than a need to label it as true or false, right or wrong.

By the time I'm completing this writing, **several years have passed since the experience I am about to describe.** It took me that long to absorb and translate it, and I have been pondering it and re-living it almost every single day since the first. **Some paragraphs may feel raw—as they were written immediately after, and they are still just as I first recorded them—while other passages and pages dive deeper, into the translations as I make sense of what I saw and felt.**

There were so many layers to move through. **At first, it was like trying to explain the effect of something based only on its taste**, while it's still just touching your tongue—like coffee, strong teas, or medicinal herbs.

An immediate description could never capture the full essence or its effects. Some things take time to understand, after they've moved through you, or once their presence has passed.

The following experience was so multifaceted and complex, that my writing may sometimes feel like a back and forth—between the rawness of the moment and the long journey of tracing each detail from its root, all the way to its far-off, corresponding leaf. Writing it all down has felt a bit like those films that shift between timelines, unfolding the intricate story back and forth through the years, until the pieces start to make sense for the viewer.

For me, every tiny part of it was pure magic, that once touched, continues to bloom, even now, through time into many vibrant petals of experience, with layers unfolding secrets of our very being, **revealing, in the end—that it is pure goodness.**

****

Remember to Remember

One summer night as I drifted off to sleep, my **determination to remember** remained as strong as it had been throughout my whole life. Considering I did not know what I forgot, the sense of loss was quite profound. I couldn't pinpoint where to begin searching. This night as I lay waiting to sleep, I repeated the familiar lines: **"Remember to remember."**

I continually asked myself: Was this sense of something missing simply loneliness? Was it a fear of missing out? Or that I needed to "find myself" and the place I was meant to be? Did I need to find my calling, my mission, my purpose? Would I even know when I had found it?

Sure, my early life had its challenges, as did most of life up to this point, but everyone has a story and I didn't feel I had it any worse then so many others, so it wasn't from that. But it always lingered in the background, and I have been out there looking, listening, and waiting for some forgotten knowledge to return.

Having an insatiable curiosity for many topics in general, has given me a hunger to understand past the fundamentals of life as we know it. It has led me to contemplate time and our existence beyond our physical bodies and minds. Thoughts of timelessness and the broader perspectives of our universe are ever present for me, regardless of what else I am doing.

Many times I wished I could just be simpler, that I could feel content and not need to ponder everything so deeply. **That I could find it in me to accept an answer someone else had already laid out, to let go of the questions and just move on.** But for the most part, I've come to view my curiosity and thirst for understanding as a privilege. Having a clear mind and a healthy energy to explore this journey of life is something I've come to treasure very much.

****

When I mention existence beyond the conscious reality we know, I don't mean this in a religious sense (and I mean no offense to anyone either.) But I've always struggled with the way organized religions often seem to **prioritize the afterlife over our current existence, encouraging us to live this life almost solely for a master plan in the next.** It is frequently believed to be a reward for those who have lived righteous lives.

This is usually accompanied by the fear of hell and, if considered worthy and well-behaved, the promise of a paradise, known by many different names: Heaven, Jannah, Sagga, Shambhala, Elysium, The Garden of Eden, and so on. There was always talk of judgment and purification, as if ones whole life was a test. Which never quite made sense to me, but I couldn't stop thinking about it all.

The version of heaven presented to me seemed like an idealized, distorted version of earthly life. One where people, **still as singular beings,** exist in a challenge-free realm that removes all discomfort. At least I believe most of these afterworlds are classically portrayed as places of all goodness, relaxation, abundance, liberation from rules and lack any form of suffering. I couldn't seem to understand how or why that would be.

On earth, we experience both heaven and hell because we suffer extreme pain as well as moments of extreme happiness and pleasure. Right here, we all can see some lives are trapped in the hell of pain and cruelty, while others live in what may be considered more of a heaven. I understand why the belief in a heaven after death is comforting and needed—especially in a world full of extremes and challenges. Religion has almost always a been part of humanity, likely because **humans have instinctively sensed something beyond the physical since the dawn of recorded history.**

In this life, who wouldn't want, and even **need,** a haven to look forward to? Health without illness, pleasure without pain, happiness and acceptance without knowing rejection or sorrow. Who wouldn't want others to love them, and never know hate? Who doesn't wish to know existence without death and who doesn't long to be reunited with their lost loved ones? But once there, would we even understand or need comfort without grief, courage or hope without fear?

The confusion or contradiction for me came from trying to imagine the afterlife as a perfect place **where we remain the same person we are now,** with our memories and identity, but in an unchallenged existence. On one hand, we know that balance and tension are necessary for growth. We know that nothing exists without its opposite. We understand that context and perspective is the only way we have to label and understand all we know on the human plain. Yet, when we think about the afterlife, we often picture it as a place beyond those contrasts—versions of our world where everything is 'all good' or 'all bad' forever.

My question has always been: how can we take who we are here, with all our human experiences and memories, to a place without the challenges and opposites that shaped us? If the afterlife has no tension, contrast or contradictions, do we remain 'ourselves'? Would we still 'recognize others'? Or do we become something entirely different? **Do we remain**

singular in the way we know it here, or do spirit and energy merge with greater unknowns once we leave our bodies?

So it came to a point where I could not believe in one specific religion, and yet I was not an atheist. But as a young adult when this true disbelief in certain things first dawned on me, I was terribly sad. I had lost a faith, and the picture of heaven that I held on to through every tough challenge I had up till then. It was lonely—**because believing something makes it real for you.** And strong *belief,* not just religious, offers a kind of companionship. It becomes an energetic, invisible ecosystem for us, something that lives with you, filters your reality, and eventually takes on a life of its own. It becomes its own quiet entity.

I still thought a lot about what lies **after** this conscious life, as well as what and where I was **prior to**, as I have already been nonexistent for all eternity before my time began.

It didn't take religion for me to know that there is more than what we experience in the here and now. I constantly sense that I am connected to something bigger, like the driver of our physical bodies and minds comes from a separate source. I am sure many people feel this, even if we can't explain it. Yet living all these years in this one body and mind can feel so limiting, so far beyond our control.

I was also always zooming out of my immediate reality, and it became a frustrating habit, but it felt like a perspective I couldn't let go of. In my mind, I would go far out into the galaxy and look back down on Earth to see how my life or any of its details might matter. I knew I was like a tiny ant. An ant with so many questions about everything.

I still carry those questions, but one day I realized: I have forever after to know what comes next. **Let us say I have death in the bag already, we all do, it's our absolute and only guarantee**, and it could arrive at any time. But while here, I want to connect to death's opposite on a more conscious level.

Knowing my time here in this specific state is extremely short has made me realize how precious it is—this tiny blur of time where I get to be conscious, with my particular collection of memories.

****

So, there I was falling asleep while I said to myself, 'remember to remember' as I had done so many times before. I was committed to bringing something new back to my current conscious reality. **And this night, it happened!**

It was about 3:30 am or so, when I entered a space I had never been able to retain in memory before. For a long time it felt like I would never be able to put it into words because getting it on paper has been extremely challenging. The experience was profoundly life-changing and was an accumulation of many small moments leading up to that night.

Before this, I had encountered what I like to call 'snippets' — small truths, flashes of alternate realities —through different cracks or patterns in our dimension. I always forgot most (but not all) of it upon waking up, except for the knowledge that I couldn't retain much of whatever it was, and I could never translate or process it into understandable thought. But the accumulation of each of those smaller experiences helped me witness and remember this, so that my mind and body retained portions of it.

If you've ever seen 'Men in Black,' you're familiar with the flashy gadget called the Neuralizer, which once flashed in your eyes, wipes out recent memories. I know it's just a movie, but that's quite often how I feel when I wake up from an experience like this. I'm aware before I wake up, that from the moment I am conscious, whatever I am experiencing will be completely erased from the memory I have access to. **It's as though it stays behind a curtain**, and what remains is only the knowledge that whatever it is will stay on the other side.

Several hours into that night, I slipped into a dimension beyond what I understood as physical life. There's no other way to describe it but to explain that it was an extended and steady bliss, like being suspended in awe.

I will say in advance, there are not words I can think to use, even now, that gives its explanation or description justice.

I will attempt to describe how it happened, as it had some similarities to a few of the previous snippets. Most of them, but not all, occurred at night, where I find myself consciously aware of my subconscious self—in a third-person sense, while being unconscious. I am fully conscious while my human brain lies unconscious, and at the same time, I am aware of them both. **Perhaps it's a split consciousness and as well as an observer.**

If, by some chance, you manage to pass through a doorway into a different dimension, it becomes exceedingly difficult to remain there for any extended period of time. This is because it contradicts the laws of our current physical world, and the limits of our human minds.

Having found myself in such places before, fully aware of what was happening, I understood that everything might vanish. Most of the time I'm reaching out, physically stretching my invisible arms as far as they can go, desperately trying to cling or hold on to that place for just a little while longer, a few more seconds even, hoping to leave a lasting imprint in my mind.

If you're a dreamer, you are familiar with those dreams where you recall the experience, but it makes no sense when you're awake. You know its right there, somewhere in your memory, but it's a blurry, nonsensical recollection. Eventually, you give up trying to remember because it's beyond your comprehension. In my case, **I understood it to be in a different code or language then my human brain knew how to process.**

****

This time, when I awoke, I wept with extreme gratitude. I was in shock and sat in astonishment. I could still see and feel it, but it took me hours to translate what I had experienced into a language my conscious mind could even begin to understand, let alone explain to anyone else. I sat there, wide awake, my mind blank, with uncontrollable tears streaming down my face, in total disbelief for the rest of the night. The following days blurred.

To retain a memory, one's consciousness needs to reside there for a significant <u>earthly</u> duration, allowing the mind to process and carry it back as a thought. Perhaps this is a fundamental law, anchoring our minds here. At first, I wrote down every single detail I could, capturing the experience in its raw form. Yet, after much time had passed, I still struggled to articulate it properly—often finding myself repeating words, sentiments, and ideas over and over because I could never do it justice. **Now, I find myself reaching for analogies, metaphors, or symbols that may provide visual examples as I attempt to explain it to others.** Nevertheless, I can still vividly envision it, and it defies any earthly comparisons. It replays daily in my mind, etched deeply in my thoughts.

Previously, I had a concept of what other dimensions might resemble, based on different versions of the forms we know in this world. My waking, and even dreaming, mind can only draw from what I've witnessed so far in this life. It can't fathom or interpret what has been entirely unfamiliar, especially when the differences and contrasts are as extreme as they were.

But where I journeyed this time was a dimension of energy— vibrant, ecstatic, joyful, and blissful, **yet utterly formless.**

FORM

I had departed from the dimension of form, arriving in a realm of pure, unadulterated energy—it was truly phenomenal and felt like I was inside whatever the atoms of bliss would be, a pure energy dimension.

I came to see, as we know, that all physical form is made up of atoms, holds energy and must vibrate at some level. That there is no such thing as 'matter with zero energy'— **but there is indeed energy with zero matter.** That's where I was.

Despite the absence of specific physical forms or solid shapes, **it was far from blank.** I felt like absolutely everything that could **be**—was there. In this formless dimension, everything coexisted harmoniously, and somehow I was experiencing it, in what seemed like full consciousness. It was a place that was vibrantly **everything and nothing simultaneously.**

In this place, I was also both everything and nothing at once. Life pulsed all around and within me—formless, stunning, overwhelming every one my senses. You know that flood of emotion that comes with **awe?** When something strikes you so deeply that you unexpectedly and involuntarily catch your breath, and your whole mind fills

with reverence?   Only this time, it wasn't just my mind—
every cell in my body felt it. My entire **being** was overcome,
as if my cells, (still back in the dimension of form), were
weeping in astonishment with me as I witnessed it there.

I realized later that, although I had left my body of form, I
could still feel it because in order for it to be a memory, it
had to be processed through my physical mind.

While there, I kept trying to name it, to understand exactly
where I was, but **how do you pin point 'everything &
nothing' when they are merged as one and the same?**

Because there were no forms, I could not discern a
specific source of light or its direction. **Yet light was there**,
permeating everything and lighting my surroundings evenly,
there were no shadows. I wasn't facing any specific
direction because there was no form to gauge myself by.

If I were to attribute colors to this place, (and I am not
completely sure that it was colors), the closest comparison
would be something like pastel shades. Countless, faint,
pastel colors drifted, billowing like visible air, as if air were
both opaque and lightly tinted in hundreds of colors, some
of them I had never seen. This soft, flowing energy filled all
space, moving with seamless grace while holding its unusual

stillness. Invisible, gentle lines—without any harsh boundaries, connected everything that existed.

Upon hearing this, I understand that a place without form might seem like—nothing—and most certainly uninteresting. For how can we possibly imagine or fix our attention on something blank? Much less talk about or attempt to explain it?

Our entire universe, as we know it, exists because of form and its opposites or polarities. **Everything we imagine here is based on what we've already seen.** In movies and books, we splice and rearrange, but it's always something familiar. We may depict aliens as giant bugs, aquatic creatures, or plants, or combine them with human form. We create beings with one, three, or a thousand eyes, or with extra limbs, but they're still based on what we know. Even the idea of no eyes is just an absence, an opposite of what we're familiar with. Whether it's a dark underworld full of imagined horrors or a paradise of all the good we can dream, everything is rooted in what we already understand.

But what I experienced took everything away from me. And yet, I was still conscious, still filled with energy, without any of the forms I know. It was extremely liberating, and anything but boring. I could never have imagined what it felt like to exist without any of the familiar markers that define the world of form. Somehow, I still sensed each cell and every atom, wherever they were, all of them ecstatic, vibrating with a kind of joy that I could feel, but not touch. **There was a sense of remembrance**—in some way it was less of a discovery and more a return to the familiar, like unlocking a door I knew somewhere I hid the key to. And now the quiet truth that had always been present washed fully over me, and I realized **I was truly missing nothing.**

****

How it felt: Most of us are familiar with the sensation of "feeling good." Now, picture the best physical sensation you can imagine. Next envision every cell in your entire body experiencing that sensation. **But here's the difference, it was not as a fleeting high or with an ultimate intensity,** which is always temporary, **but as a sustained and tranquil <u>state</u> of being,** calmly and perpetually, without any 'up's' or 'down's'. It just was.

There are levels beyond form and beyond our senses. These levels or fields, are **not beyond in terms of physical space or location necessarily, but are interlaced with the tangible and visible things.** An essence or state of being that exists there with the physical, yet operating on different planes.

I saw that even our understanding of space is conditioned by form. We can't conceive of a place where 'space' doesn't matter—because here, we measure it in relation to matter. We ask: What fills it? How much fits? We calculate capacity, boundaries, emptiness, and fullness—all defined by what's there. But in the formless realm, space didn't seem to matter. There was nothing to measure. Without form, there's no need for boundaries. It was all one and the same—continuous, inseparable, and unbroken.

Without form, space may not act like a container. Distance becomes irrelevant—there's nothing to separate. I know that is very hard for our minds to grasp—at least it is for mine. But, I experienced it personally and after, it occurred to me that perhaps this innate sense of something beyond space and form is what humans have always tried to describe through religion—the idea of a god or spirit that is everywhere at once. In that formless realm, such a concept actually makes perfect sense. Because it exists beyond the rules of form.

I don't know how, and I may never fully understand it, but **this place was filled with a void so profound that, somehow, it held everything within it,** and was revealed to me in a way I could witness and experience. Throughout the entire time there, I never lost awareness of my earthly body and that it was highly probable I might not carry it back with me as a memory this time.

****

TIME

I was also aware that, in terms of earthly time, it had only been a few seconds, perhaps just two or so. However, I experienced it as a slow, drawn-out event without any sense of urgency. **Time, in this place, simply did not exist, so it did not matter how much time it was equal to.**

Describing the feeling of being conscious, in a timeless realm, while retaining an awareness of time in the physical world is quite challenging. I knew earth would pull me back into the flow of time. But while in that dimension, I remained in a timeless 'now' and although it won't make any sense to say this, I was there, without hurry, for a long amount of time.

Afterwards, I thought 'How could there possibly be anywhere that time does not exist?' I've always been deeply intrigued by the concept and mystery of time. I have pondered it a lot. Sometimes even challenged it to meet me face to face. I've written poems about it, spent hours in nature thinking about time, trying to grasp what it really is. But something always just felt out of my reach. This experience though, helped me understand it in a way I hadn't before.

Time is measured by change, or seen as the measured duration of something. Without a physical world of form to mark or track passages, and without anything capable of physically changing or evolving, time loses its meaning. Form, and its changes, together create what we know as time.

While I was there in this formless dimension, it became clear that **without form, time is nil.** In fact, without a conscious mind to measure it, without human perception, time becomes irrelevant.

When consciousness joins with form, it assumes the limitations of form. A silent countdown begins. Not measurable in the moment because we can't know our end, yet it is always moving. We can't track it precisely while living, but we live with the awareness that the clock is ticking. **This is awareness—the understanding that all form must eventually (and possibly at any time) change and begin to dissolve. Therefore, time and awareness are inseparable.**

Time is a property of the universe that describes the relationships and changes of form within it. **Time is a dimension but is is not a separate entity or something that exists on its own.** It cannot be stored or transferred, it is more like a support or field, that allows changes in form to be measured. Kind of like how the color of an object is not an existence on its own, but is a property that is seen only by the interaction of light and matter.

Another example is temperature, it doesn't exist as an independent thing. Time is a measure of the relationships and changes occurring in the universe, but it doesn't act or exist independently from those changes. **Consider time, color and temperature as comparable concepts, they are not standalone entities.** Time needs a mind to perceive or measure the changes in form, just as color requires eyes and light to see it, and temperature needs matter to hold or express it. They are all properties of physical systems, and **without matter or the structure of form, they would not exist.**

And while considering perception—and the fact that we can measure time, see color, feel temperature, and experience countless aspects of existence—it naturally led me next to the question of purpose. Why us?

****

Why are we here? Why do we have minds that measure, observe, remember and remain aware of it all? Everything else in nature has a traceable purpose. Although of course the magnitude of this arrangement is truly beyond our human comprehension, no matter how much we study it. But, take for example, even a small weed that may live for only a couple of days. In its short existence, it spreads seeds, feeds insects or birds, and contributes to the ecosystem in ways that ripple through the inter-connected circles and web of life. In nature, almost nothing exists for itself alone, it is all connected to something else.

We are part of nature, but what role do we play in earths cycles? We humans seem to stand apart. Unlike other living beings, (as far as we know) we are the creatures that carry individual consciousness. We can watch and question ourselves and our actions. **And throughout countless generations, we have indeed questioned our purpose.**

We have written records containing these existential questions of our purpose, going back 4,000-5,000 years. And before written findings, we have ritual and symbolic evidence suggesting existential awareness possibly even 100,000 years ago. So this curiosity, **this question we all carry** for understanding our purpose, seems to be as old as humanity itself. It is something that comes from deep within our consciousness. **That persistent question suggests it must hold valid significance—otherwise, why would it continually arise in us at all, all over the world?**

In nature, purpose is often clear. Each organism fits into a delicate, traceable balance. But **nothing** else in nature questions its own purpose the way we do. So while it's tempting (for simplicity's sake) to believe human life just exists without deeper meaning, to believe we are, and then are not, we still can't seem to let go of the need to seek purpose—to explain why we're here at all.

I've heard the following said many times, in different ways — "Humans are not needed on Earth. The Earth would be much better off without us. Maybe we **should** die off. Maybe that's what we deserve. " It's the kind of thought that seeps in and makes you feel guilty for simply existing and for needing anything at all. It certainly makes one feel bad about human advancements. But thankfully, another voice also rises up, the one that remembers: **"Hey, we are nature too. We are life. We are a one-of-a-kind species."** And like the pine tree, the dandelion, the lion, the eagle, the fish, or the tiny drifting plankton—we also belong here. If not we wouldn't be here.

So now, after this experience, I see it differently, and it's beautiful. **We are the eyes through which creation witnesses itself.** And like all living things, our role is not extinction, but continuation. Our task isn't to question whether we deserve to remain. It's to live our experiences with reverence. To honor the chance we get to be present and aware, and give it our best, no matter the jungle, desert or mountain we find ourselves in.

****

EXPERIENCE

All this brings us to 'experience'. **There isn't one single purpose that fits all; purpose is unique to each of us because <u>we are experience incarnate.</u>**

Purpose, like time, only exists when observed. It cannot exist independently from the searching mind, just as time exists only because we observe and measure it, settling on a determined value. <u>Without an observer, what meaning can there be in an event, an object, or a moment?</u> Meaning isn't inherent in things themselves; it lies only in our awareness, existing only when and if we seek it.

Purpose, then, is not something that exists out there, hanging around and waiting to be discovered. **It is a creation**, born from our desire to give meaning to the finite bodies we inhabit, to the temporary journey we are experiencing.

We search for and settle on purposes because we are creators, and **the act of creating is as vital to us as breathing.** It is through the creation of 'purpose' that we attempt to understand the very nature of our existence. We create to make sense of a world bound by time and limitation, because our creative minds are bursting with the desire to break free of that constraint. **Purpose is like a loving and caring touch for our souls. It soothes us through hardships, for when you settle on a purpose, you can endure any challenge.**

We are the creator species. The only species that imagines, and builds whatever massive plans we first see in the mind. We don't just adapt to the world—we reshape it with thought, intention, and the power to turn the unseen into form. **We create by choice, not just instinct.** We carry within our minds, a profound and magnificent construct of nature. One that is aware enough to witness and question itself (when allowed to grow in this direction).

It's as though life, in all its wonder and growth, wanted to witness its own unfolding—so we were born.

We are the physical carriers of experience itself—the embodiment of experience. Naturally, we each see only a narrow slice of existence through our own perspectives. But, within the infinite space of reality, we are all connected, everything exists, and every possibility has its place. Because experience is shaped by countless ongoing variations, free will for us is essential—allowing every version of life's unfolding to take shape, just as the rest of existence does.

To add to the challenge of it all, our world of form is one of opposites, and we ourselves embody that very nature. With our awareness, we feel the duality within us, and that often **creates a sense of tension.** We are so much more than our physical bodies can contain, yet we are anchored to this world by form. What drives the mind, however, knows no limits.

As a result, we live with a constant contradiction: the timeless energy within us is housed in bodies that are finite. **We are—as life is—both sides of the coin,** we are the infinite and the finite, and because of this, the part of us that is timeless, will always feel like a question, to the part of us that is limited by form. The 'why's' will always linger in the background of our minds. But, these opposites are necessary and come together to create experience through us.

'Experience' is a uniquely human phenomenon that does not have a simple categorization. With each of us as creators, we continually add to our own reality, every moment contributing to life's variety and continuity. **Experience grows and collects into itself, shaped by the perceptions we choose—*"each of us a gear that turns another, even as another turns us."*** (From my book *Poetry Dust*) This all creates the wild and un-scriptable game of life experience.

And, oh how we experience. We scale **emotional** highs that feel as high as the andes, where from emotion alone our hair may stand on its ends and our heads may spin. And we can plunge into lows as deep as the Mariana Trench, where the invisible weight of everything in our minds threatens to collapse us. Our emotions can surge like invisible tidal waves, flooding every corner of our being, making us feel like our emotions are way too large for our fragile, human forms to contain.

The whole world seems to hold its breath with us when we stand in awe of beauty or in the presence of those we love. Yet, we are also capable of suffering so profound it seems to travel beyond our own existence. We hold the key to feeling nearly everything this world has to offer, from incredible joy to the hardest of sorrows. **And, we were never meant to experience only one side of anything in this life.**

In fact, I believe that **when life becomes too easy for too long, humans tend to unconsciously create new problems, as if they are restless for something more.** It's not the problems themselves they seek, but the depth, challenge, and contrast that make life feel meaningful and make us feel worthy. An innate need to experience the full range of existence. Humans will always want to see if there is more, even if it comes with struggles—**we are always searching for the balance of all things, and for all we can be.**

The Challenges of Human Experience in a World of Form and Opposites

Of course, human life is and will always be challenging. Some times more than others, but this is natural, just as in nature. There are times of peaceful weather and the perfect temperature, where all flourishes and grows easily, and times of storm, flood, fire, and drought.

As much as we would like to have only the good side, and while we can make ourselves believe we **deserve** only good or at least ease, during this lifetime—**experience itself requires contrast.**

Everything in the world of form has its opposite, and I know I mentioned this earlier, but WE, as conscious beings, don't just encounter opposites—**we embody them.** We juggle countless contradictions within ourselves for as long as we live.

The greatest contradiction of all is the one we carry from birth: that we are alive, and yet bound to die. **No matter where or how we're born—into riches or hardship, beauty, struggle, lack or luck—none of us outrun the one truth we all share: death comes for everyone**, and it seldom sends word ahead. Not knowing our endpoint is an awareness that quietly shapes nearly everything we do.

This paradox—this contrast of opposites—this is what makes the human journey so intense, and so precious. **We are the great contradiction and aware of it.** We are fire and water, both vehicle and driver, child and guardian.

We are the ones who see, and the ones being seen. We are the witnesses, and the ones being witnessed. We are the knowers, and the known.

We carry the past with us every day, through memory and form, yet we can never move backward—only forward. We are the infinite breath contained within finite form. **It is precisely this tension, this merging of opposites with awareness, that allows experience to exist at all.**

As I ponder "experience," a flood of them returns to me. Somehow, in my not-so-long life, I've already gathered a decent variety. I'm sure many can relate to the changes experienced when reflecting on one's life so far.

I've known hunger—the kind that makes you wonder if you'll ever stop worrying how to feed yourself or your children. And I've also known full cupboards, and the heaviness of being stuffed, eating more than needed, where digestion feels like hours of work. I've felt love in all its grandeur and balance—and I've watched it twist into obsession, dangerous in its extremes. I've been abused, unsure how to think for myself or escape what felt unfixable. And I've stood on my own ground, strong, in control of my life.

I've lived in the tropics without air conditioning and often electricity, sweat pouring endlessly under a burning sky, where your skin feels like prickling fire. And I've endured subfreezing winters without proper clothing, dreaming of warmth returning to my bones. For many years, I fit everything I owned into one suitcase—and I've also filled houses so full that it took months to let it all go when moving. I've owned brand new vehicles—and cars I couldn't take on the freeway for fear they'd catch fire.

I've been loved, and I've been abandoned. I've felt loneliness so deep it physically hurt—and I've known deep, safe companionship. I've witnessed birth and given birth. I've felt the sharp, crushing, pain of death. I've felt lost and I've felt found. **The creature that I am has been blown like particles—through cities, across borders, over mountains, through valleys, to the sea.** Living in tents, shacks, and mansions.

I look back on my childhood and past as if they were a treasure box, holding gold, diamonds, and elixirs, as well as poison, daggers, and blood.

In remembering them all, I try to calm the waters of my soul —to remind myself that nothing is permanent, which helps slow the waves of reaction when times are difficult. It allows me to guide the tides of emotion as they rise over life's many changing situations.

When I line up all these moments—and many more, so many sides of so many coins—I see the common thread: it's me, experiencing life. And with that, I feel immense gratitude for the fullness of it all—for how life, in both everything and nothing, in lack and in plenty, tries to teach me to remember the balance of all things.

****

Upon returning and reuniting with my physical body, it felt like I was in very slow motion. My arms reached forward, grasping for just a bit more time in that extraordinary place. For a slow but brief moment, I was aware of traveling through my spine, beginning from my lower back and moving upwards, then to my neck, it was odd but I knew exactly in my body where I was, bones, muscle, tissue and everything, and then just like that—in a flash I was back.

Oh how desperately I wished for more time to absorb it and understand a little better. As I awoke, I wept — tears of happiness and gratitude. I sobbed. I couldn't stop crying at the fact that I had experienced formlessness and timelessness, and that I had brought back with me a few seconds of that eternity. My feelings were a mix of excitement, happiness, relief, shock and complete, blissful awe. I was determined to retain and interpret everything I could.

In an attempt to explain this, I have used words like 'beyond' and 'there' to convey that I was in a different reality, but it was the same location as my physical presence, though everything appeared different. **In essence, I didn't have to travel to a new location;** I simply was conscious, within a different vibrational dimension.

Now that I've visited that place, and can recall and feel what it was like; the memory of being there is imprinted in my every cell. **We are one with the nonphysical, and we are 'everything and nothing' in both time-bound and timeless states.**

****

WORDS

Once back, the very first words that came to mind, and the only way I could **initially** explain it, even to myself, were that I was the 'definition' of the words. — **I felt like I was 'one with the words.'** **And at that point of interpreting the experience, this really threw me off.** Why would it manifest or translate in my mind as being 'one with the words'? What words? What did words have to do with any of this? I began to record which words they were.

Since then, I have had to think long and hard about words. **What are they? Since I had no words yet to explain it with—no language, it felt ineffable.** My mind and imagination were at an impasse, as if I were standing at the edge, the crack between imagination and thought. Without words, I just couldn't fully grasp it; my understanding seemed to stop where my language failed me, remaining unknown, as the ability to process it was missing. And yet, it was right there, still sharing space with me.

I just needed to translate it into words, to be able to shape it into thoughts, so my mind could comprehend it. **I had to get it to the stage of words.**

Words are tangible vessels because they are carriers of something deeply intangible—thoughts. They give form to the formless, they are vehicles through which the abstract can become concrete. And what are thoughts but unshaped potential, links between the seen and the unseen. They are a bridge, connecting and merging the formless with matter— or at least with what could and will become matter.

Of course, thoughts do not exist in isolation. I suppose they emerge from our collective memories, from awareness perhaps born of the 'collective unconscious'. From the unknown yet ever familiar, living energy that fills us all. How many of our thoughts came from the collective memories of those before us or around us? We can't ever truly know. And yet, once we receive them and allow them in, they are born a-new, continually shaped by perception. I realize that consciousness is a subjective experience, its interpretation varies depending on perspective—whether we are viewing life through scientific, philosophical, or spiritual lenses. But when all form dissolves, when boundaries end, do separations of energy merge together into something incomprehensible for us?

I struggled to understand the difference between 'words' and 'thoughts'- how to separate where one ends and the other begins, and the order of silent thought.

Can thoughts exist before words? Some thoughts arrive quickly to fully formed language, maybe those are an accumulation, not exactly new ideas. Because others start as a sensation, reaction, emotion, or formless knowing—things we are on the verge of grasping but cannot yet name. Words may not create thought, but they shape it, they give it structure and define it. Once put into words, a thought is no longer what it was before, yet thoughts remain fluid, always open to the evolution we give them.

Nonetheless, these are the supports that exist for us and ones we need: subconsciousness to awareness, to structuring thoughts, and **simultaneously to the formation of words**—allowing us to fully participate in the experience of conscious life. They maintain our connection to the unseen, to the intangible part of ourselves that merges with the laws of form.

Would we still wonder who we are if we had no words? Without language, expanded thought remains silent and perhaps even dormant. Our awareness would become immediate or reactive rather than reflective, unable to reach deeper layers of self-exploration or any abstract thought. **It is through language that we refine, expand, and shape awareness into something more than instinct.** Without words, we could not contemplate existence, time, philosophical thought, or the nature of our being.

I wanted to grasp this realization about words fully. Even before this experience, I had always been deeply intrigued by Helen Keller's story. (I know, who isn't?) Helen Keller, who was deaf and blind from a young age, described her pre-language world as formless and without self. In her own words: *"Before my teacher came to me, I was like an animal... I did not know that I am. I lived in a world that was a no-world."* In her case, it was only through the breakthrough of tactile language that her awareness expanded into memory, meaning, and abstract thought.

That first *aha* moment, when she famously made the connection between water flowing over her hands and the letters W-A-T-E-R—was a breakthrough transformation for her. After that, with a teacher and access to symbolic language, her thinking expanded quite rapidly. All this aligned deeply with what I was beginning to understand, that words allow us to access the layers of consciousness we so often take for granted.

That realization about words opened, or maybe connected something else for me, an abstract thought I had carried even before the experience, something I hadn't know where to place until now.

****

An abstract thought: A slip in the crack

This short sentence, *'a slip in the crack'* is something I had been reflecting on for a few years prior to the experience of **Two Seconds of Eternity**. It came to me due to a few surreal visions or glimpses I had experienced.

I began to feel that everything new that enters this world of form must pass through a physical opening, a crack, to get here. I know how strange and perhaps even insignificant or obvious that sounds. But this may apply even to the non tangible. If we look closely, doesn't everything come into being through some kind of physical opening?

Birth itself is the most obvious example. But whether human, animal, or plant, life emerges through a passage, a rupture, a break into our now— from what came before. A seed splits before it grows. Water can find its way into life only through openings—through cracks in the earth, slipping through the smallest fractures and open crevices, spilling through unseen gaps. Even breath, what sustains us every second, must pass continually through an opening to fill the lungs, entering through the nose and mouth, and continuing our life with each inhale. Sound also must find a way in. Vibrations traveling through openings, reaching us only when there is space for them to pass through.

Everything living is filled with, and shaped by, cracks. Life itself is porous. It all requires fractures, breaks, cracks and entryways. Nothing new takes form in our world except through an opening. Skin, roots, lungs, and cells all allow for movement, breath, and transformation. Even at the smallest level, pores are gateways—tiny openings in our skin that regulate temperature, and in plants, their tiny pores help them open and close, exchanging what is needed to make photosynthesis possible.

Life simply does not exist in a sealed state. It requires passage and exchange, a way for what is within to connect to what is beyond. **To be alive is to be open in some way, to take in and to release. To pass through life and to be passed through by life.**

But I never considered the invisible things, until now. I wasn't sure how they arrived. I assumed that because they were not bound by form, they would just somehow appear here, and wouldn't require an opening, a crossing, a passageway, or a breach—to reach us.

I think even what is invisible to our eyes, **if it is to enter the world of form,** must pass through an opening between worlds. Things we can't see—like a thought, a breath, or the breeze—still require passage. Air, for instance, expands only into available space. Chemical reactions too, require something to break—bonds that shift, separate, and reform to allow a new form to emerge.

Thoughts seem to rise through an opening in the mind, a crack in the pattern of what was. There must be a point they cross. Thoughts must cross this barrier before they can enter a mind that functions in the world of form.

In the unseen processes, could it be that, just like in nature, things only emerge when something opens? Do ideas, knowledge, and change—whether visible or not—require a breach, a passage, a slip in the crack, a shift, before they can take form? **Everything here needs an entry point, a doorway where the formless becomes form, where potential crosses into existence.** This experience seemed to exist in the space between, where raw impressions begin to stir before thoughts can take shape into words. **An in-between where language hasn't yet defined its meaning, yet something is undeniably taking place.**

Maybe even love needs an opening. It's always searching for spaces and cracks to enter. That's why you can offer love to someone, but if there's no space in them to receive it, it won't yet take root.

****

THE DEFINITIONS OF

W ell, although at that time, it did not make immediate sense, I felt the gravity of words and began to document it exactly as it first translated and unfolded in my mind.

The most important words I was the "definition of " were:
Bliss - Peace - Air - Silence - Nothing - Everything - Love - Joy

There was no presence of fear, anxiety, worry, stress, or evil —no concern or sadness in any form. All the energy somehow exuded a sense of well-being and safety. I was actually looking around to search for its opposites, for anything negative, but it was simply not there.

I was whole and complete. **Because all was nothing—there was nothing to divide.** All guilt, judgments, opinions and labels had vanished and wouldn't have mattered anyways. **I simply was and without question.** I had never felt that free in my whole life. How could I have? I was completely weightless, as if inside the atoms of unadulterated life energy.

I could see how all these words were in a timeless category. But some of them I needed to reflect on, to see how they were in the same group as the others.

The words LOVE, JOY and BLISS for example, were things my waking mind would not normally have associated in the same group as some of the other words. I had deemed those as emotions, and the other words were more like elements, compounds, mixtures or absences. Yet the more I reflected on it, in that place, they were all the same. **And it very soon became abundantly clear, that the strongest pull of any of these, was love.**

Love was absolutely everything, and it was impossible to be the energy of love without being joy and thus bliss and everything else. In this state, they were all one, they were a unified essence. Love here, was as tangible as water or as ever constant, natural and present as air, as all surrounding as particles and atoms are in this world. **It was an essential element of everything in life as we know it.**

Trust me, I was taken by surprise by this. And I understand that it probably sounds very cliché or like a message from a sermon, but it is not. **Rather, I think these words have been often misunderstood**, and we tend to think of them differently than they truly are. It was not LOVE for something or someone, and it was not JOY because of anything specific or the result of a situation or occurrence.

<u>Love was the force itself.</u> It was an essential element of existence, like breathing air. Love was all-encompassing. I truly had considered love and joy as "emotions"—we attach love to feelings, then assign them to something or someone in the physical world, a habit formed because we are of physical form. Breaking free from this mentality of holding love only as a result of someone or something would be challenging, however a new goal was born in me to explore how I could implement this.

The more I thought about it, 'love' emerged as such a profoundly loaded word, it just grew and grew like expansive and hungry roots seeking water. There is so much that lives within that one thing. By centering attention solely on being more love, it would bring out numerous other virtues. Such as inclusion, protection, affection, care, commitment, sacrifice, patience, acceptance, kindness, tenderness, generosity, compassion, selflessness, understanding, empathy, UNITY and the capacity to forgive often.

Not only does love give, but it balances as it takes away. Love can override hate, vengeance, bitterness and anger. Positivity and optimism are manifestations of love for life and happiness. **In essence, all these qualities are simply different facets of love.** But I rather appreciated how one word could encompass all of this, instead of trying to label the different kinds of love or additional explanations it seems to deserve. It simplified my constant personal lists of **"needs work on"**, because **if I focus on this one thing**, I can grow in many useful and worthy ways.

EMOTIONS

After this experience, I became more aware of emotions and how **we often allow them to become toxic** all on our own, albeit unintentionally.

In that place, I had been freed from all labels and felt completely weightless, untouched by emotion—an experience that's difficult to explain in words. **But as I returned to my body that night, emotions quickly settled back in, like being covered by a thick, iron blanket.** All the labels, attachments, fears, regrets, guilt, and responsibilities poured back into me like molten lead. **As my memories returned**, they stacked upon each other, each layer piling on quickly, until I could hardly move beneath the weight of emotion. **I remembered the violence of war, the suffering and injustices of the world, and my own traumas, responsibilities, and regrets—each one adding to the crushing heaviness.** So tremendous was the weight, I could not physically move as I absorbed what was happening.

I understood clearly that emotions are an essential part of being human, allowing us to fully experience life.

Yet, since emotions had settled back into my body as if they were an extremely heavy weight, I saw how necessary it is to develop more control over them, and for my mind to act in my best interest, rather than allowing my own tendencies to work against me, as they frequently do. It would do us all well to be taught (and learn from a young age) how to take full responsibility for our own emotions, **versus the habit of blaming others or every circumstance for how we feel.** After all, who else could be in control of them? That is one of the things that is ours alone to master. No one else can feel or know exactly what we feel. So learning the inner workings of our minds should be a top priority.

It occurred to me that perhaps there's a way for our opposite emotions to work together somehow, as they are versions of each other—by showing each negative emotion its opposite when needed, like holding up a mirror. There's something freeing in that balance.

Isn't that in itself almost inconceivable in terms of explaining what we can do? The idea that I can take one of my emotions—which operates even beneath the radar of thought, invisible, intangible, flexible, and ever-changing— and show it to its opposite? It's quite surreal.

Well it turns out, it's not always easy to identify the opposite emotion **when you're in the thick of reaction.** But if you can do so, it, helps in clarifying what you are truly feeling. Sometimes, I need to take my anger, frustration or fear, all parts of me—and introduce them to their counterpoints, which are also part of me. **When they meet I often feel instantly calmer, and find balance as I'm reminded that I am still whole.** I can work on the habit of not letting suffering take over so completely. I simply can't forget how heavy emotions settled back in to me. It was shocking, but very clear.

I'm not saying in any way that we should be robotic or numb. Emotions are how we grow in connection, care and understanding others. But certain negative emotions when allowed to remain persistently, take heavy root and become a part of us. Then we lose our control. **We must pay attention to the emotions we feed** and ask if they align with who we even want to be. The balance we need isn't 'out there' somewhere, it is always inside of us.

I bear no illusions that this life event I witnessed means I'll now remain in some state of bliss or ease. **Not in the slightest.** I know I must fully embody and embrace physical existence as a whole, not wasting anything that experience brings my way.

****

These few seconds of eternity, spent in the absence of this life's most basic fundamentals (form), placed me beyond the normal frameworks of life as I was used to. I was inside a liminal space that liberated me of everything. To this day, it has left me with a never-ending spring of life-changing reflections and a conviction of all the goodness that is a part of us.

In that absence, I began to understand things that had once felt incomprehensible. **Not because anything was added, but because everything else was stripped away.** You can keep adding and adding to an equation, trying to solve it, but sometimes it's the subtraction that reveals the answer. **And when all that remained was love, it revealed itself as the most essential truth of all. We are here to experience form, and in doing so, to reveal love as its greatest expression.**

Some things had become crystal clear: **Our current dimension is the realm of form and therefore, of time, which brings about the dimension of opposites and everything that form entails.** Polarities or dualities are inherent to life as we know it, and we will always have the opposite side of everything that exists in our universe.

As much as we try, **we will never erase opposites from this world.** We will never eliminate pain, suffering, hate, or war, just as we will always have their opposites—joy, pleasure, peace and most importantly, love. The only way through this game, is in the balance.

Each of us enters life filled with the earth of a dormant garden, holding within us the seeds of every possibility. And 'all that's watered, grows'—a line I first wrote in *Poetry Dust*, and one I remember frequently as I comb through my own thoughts and habits.

We water a seed (symbolic of any possibility) each time we give it attention or energy.

As good and evil each spreads their seeds, humanity fans the winds, sending them far and wide. **And even if we don't experience extreme contrasts or the horrors of life personally, we *feel* them through empathy and imagination.** We read about them, hear them, catch their whispers, and absorb them through the headlines, films, screens and stories that shape our collective and expanding imaginations. **We each spread our own thoughts no less than a flower spreads its pollen.** And in this, humanity continues to grow its possibilities through each other. Both the good and the bad.

All of this affects us in our walk through life as the botanical gardens that we are—blooming with good, with harm, and with all that grows in between on the path of experience. **It all begins with the duality that form brings.**

Another realization was that I was not there in this incredible and accepting place because of something I did or did not do on earth. There was a certain anxiety I carried from many different influences and the world in general, of whether or not I was good enough—good enough for my own life, for others, worthy enough for God and whatever the afterlife was. It feels like a constant judging. Is everyone pleased with my choices? So even when I put all that aside and stepped away from mainstream thinking, it would still creep up in me, like "what if I am wrong about everything? What if some kind of judgment is waiting?" It was looming.

But this, this was a non-physical, integral part of who I was regardless of my human self, although how much I stay connected and remember this part of me would indeed depend on my daily choices and habits.

I found myself immersed in profound peace, **as if for a moment, all had been solved.** But even that peace showed me how much our experiences depend on the contrasts of this life. Because relief only exists in relation to tension.

"Solving" something is only meaningful if there is something to solve. They don't work without each other.

But still, for the first time, the deep longing and aching within me, the part that had always struggled to 'remember to remember'—had abated. I thought I might never comprehend it, but I had touched it and brought back a tiny fragment. And it was a lot.

All boundaries between what I thought was "me" and "everything else" were dissolved, and I was part of the whole, which at that level was the same as nothing specifically, because it was everything—it was beyond labels.

Without form, I had no conflicting thoughts, no time, no past or future, no labels. I was the before and after, as one. **It was whatever made atoms and energies collide, pre- and post-existence, all woven into one profound experience.**

There exists a dimension of solid bliss that we are all a part of. We have the capacity to tap into this extraordinary place or, **at the very least, become aware that it is always a part of us.**

****

How a Full Spectrum of All That Is, Is Born

I had once thought eternity was some far off promise, sealed beyond the incomprehensible world of time. But it came to me in a flash—and it was beautiful. It might have been only two seconds or so of earthly time, and yet in that timeless experience, I glimpsed the structure of my life through its absence, and felt the infinite current of love moving through it all.

I saw how we enter this world of form through pure goodness, and how the existence of form itself creates a counterpart to everything—even if only through its absence. **In this realm of duality, the moment goodness appears, the possibility of its opposite—evil—must also exist.**

From these two extremes, the full spectrum of human experience is born—every emotion, every intention, every reaction, and possibility in between.

Individually and collectively, the more we love, the more love grows. The more we hate, the more hate grows. **And so it is with all things.**

Good and evil, as opposing sides, are not abstract ideas reserved for a distant spirit world or an afterlife. Rather, they are fundamental forces created and experienced here, in this life, as part of the duality inherent in the world of form.

The laws of form that bring these dualities are not punishment or doctrine, they do not exist beyond the physical. They belong to, and are conditions of us, through the expression of <u>form</u>. It is here, through our consciousness and awareness, that we observe and experience these polarities, label them, contribute to them, and try to make sense of it all as best we can.

We, the creatures born to create and experience, flourish with all that is good—and we are also the ones who bring evil into form. We stretch both of these to their extremes, riding every wave of the spectrum in between, carrying them with us to the ends of our existence.

Nothing else in nature knows evil. It does not act from malice but from the instinct to survive and continue life. Nature kills not to cause suffering, but to perpetuate itself. It takes only what is needed to grow—never out of vengeance or greed. It does not envy the fate or abundance of another tree, bird, or beast. Even in death, it leaves behind the seeds of new life, ensuring the cycle of its continuance.

Nature's destruction is never cruel—it is the rhythm of change that brings in new beginnings. It burns, floods, and breaks, but always rebuilds. Forests prone to fire grow trees with serotinous cones, their seeds waiting to be released only by the heat of a flame. The fire does not end these forests; it begins them anew. Like a snake shedding its skin, growth requires leaving the old behind.

From the outside, not all growth is visible. We won't always understand why changes happen. Some changes begin in the dark, under the surface, and on timelines we may not be aware of. Like the violence of the sea, shaping the shore for nature's own reasons, growth often takes place outside of our understanding, always pushing towards transformation and renewal.

Nature flaps its wings, blooms its seeds, births its young, sheds its cocoons—all with the same grace with which it dies. For both the lion and the lamb are sacred, and we would not call the lion evil.

Human experience, in all its complexity, is no less a part of nature than the changing tides or the hunger of the lion. But we are different creatures, whose complicated emotions give rise to vastly different scenarios. We attempt to make sense of what is just or unjust. Yet, when we look back across thousands of years, it's clear—we haven't found a way to eliminate the harmful seeds from the hearts of humanity. This is because we carry within us the seeds of every possibility—each one awakened by the contrast of our ongoing choices and experiences.

The polarities of human existence cannot be erased, for they are inherent to what we are. We can fight them, but we must also accept them if we want to understand why we are what we are, and why humanity does what it does. Accepting the complexities of human nature—including both its positive and negative aspects—is essential for deeper understanding and, ultimately, **the progress of our collective experience.**

But like time, evil and harm do not await us in the afterlife. They live in our awareness here. While we may not be able to eliminate the polarities within our hearts and minds, we must each attempt to live morally. Not out of fear of distant judgment, hell, or the afterlife, but to nourish the good within us and shape the world we share and experience, now. **That is the only way love gains ground.**

Because each of our choices, daily, conscious, and personal, is what shapes the realities of our world. Even with the understanding of all that is, we must strive to create as much love on earth as we can. When hell comes knocking, as it sometimes will, we can meet it with a heaven so fierce, so sure, so radiant, we refuse to die inside it.

This is the responsibility and the privilege of being human: to build on what we know to be good. Not in name or theory, not in the labels we adopt or ideals we speak of for others, but through how **we** chose to live and the standard we uphold for our own actions. **To embody love even in the face of its opposite. For in this world of form, with its endless dance of dualities, our own transformation is the only change we can truly control.**

When all the beliefs and opinions about others' actions are stripped away, it comes down to this for me: Do I bring heaven or hell to all those whom life has placed in my path?

Each of us is a contributor—every day, to pain or peace, to fear or love, to division or unity. The world of form may require opposites, but we are the ones who build on those choices. **It begins and ends with what we choose to focus on, water, and grow.**

In the brief time we're given, we become the creators of experience—the ones who bloom love or sow harm, for ourselves, for each other, and for our part in this world of all that is.

****

As for words, they move between the formless and the formed. They belong to both realms but remain in neither, which is what makes them timeless. Words act as invisible carriers of consciousness. Language shapes how we think, bringing and delivering what could, and often will, become tangible. Words are powerful, essential components of all we have come to be. I couldn't comprehend the experience without words to describe it, and I began to see just how deeply the entire human experience depends on words.

Yet even if parts of these understandings never reach the clarity that words can offer, love—and the wholeness of all that is—still lives within us. **It is a part of us, like a creature of breath, a steady undercurrent in the ocean of cells that hold us in form.**

Because love, unlike form, is not bound by physical law, yet we are a home for its expression. We embody it, seek it, lose it and search to rediscover it. We need it. I realized after this that **even if all we do within our lives is live fiercely for and with love, it is enough—our lives will grow.** Without love, humanity would destroy itself. Love is the reason, the force, and the joy that keeps us alive.

****

Realizing that when we leave these bodies, we return only to the love, goodness, and unity of all that is—was a beautiful feeling. To know that death is a relief, a letting go, a return to bliss, and that there is no suffering beyond the world of form, revealed something profound: freedom. The only true freedom, in fact—because **real freedom can only exist when it is no longer needed.**

Saying this might sound to some as though I carry a negativity about this life, but that's not it at all. To the contrary, every minute here, with all its contrasts, is a treasure—and I'm in no hurry to leave. As I've said before, death and eternity are already ours, guaranteed.

In those few seconds of eternity, I didn't receive instructions or answers.   I was simply shown something vital: that we need the order and the chaos, the stillness and the noise, the pain and the joy. Duality is not the enemy of unity: it is its expression. Without the contrast brought from opposites, nothing can be understood.

Without form, there would be no reflection. Without words, no bridge to awareness. **Without love, no reason for any of this to matter. Love holds even the strongest opposites in its hands.**

The human experience—messy, challenging, and miraculous as it is—is not a detour that keeps us from discovering meaning; it *is* the meaning. It's all happening here and always, now. Expressing itself in the swing of life's pendulum, in breath, in emotion, in words, in form, and always through us.

Love is the strongest force we can nurture.
We are born from it, and we shall return to it,
for it is the essence of our being.

No matter where we come from, love is the one thing we can
all hold close, even in the face of life's hardest trials. Even
when justice, abundance, or peace seem absent,
love endures.

**Timeless and divine, love is that which connects us all
—it is ever-present, waiting for all who are ready to
embrace its power and light.**

Thank you for taking the time to read *Two Seconds of Eternity*. I hope this exploration of time, existence, and the unseen has offered you something meaningful—whether a new insight, a reflection, or a new sense of wonder. As we experience time through consciousness, may our forever-now allow us to explore, evolve, and **embrace the boundless potential of love, which runs through each of us like a current.**

Additional Insights

EMOTIONAL OPPOSITES CHART

In Case of Overwhelm: For the quiet or loud moments, and for anyone who might find this helpful, I've made a list of difficult emotions as I experience them, to better pinpoint what's overwhelming me. **Once I identify the feeling, I shift my focus to its opposites,** which helps me calm down and process what I'm feeling. **It's the ideal balance I'm searching for.**

I keep these opposites on a small index card because, in moments of overwhelm, it's easy to forget them. **If I'm overwhelmed by one emotion, I've lost the middle ground, and that imbalance tips me over.** I search for any opposite feeling I've experienced, even briefly, and bring it to the front of my mind. I introduce the emotions to each other and remind myself that I exist in the space between them both, and that I am always whole.

The calming emotion always wins—**not by suppressing or shaming its opposite, but by restoring balance and allowing harmony between them.** We all know that a calm mind brings clarity far better than stress ever could.

You can create your own list, but below is mine so far:

Angry – Calm, Peaceful, Accepting, Serene
Betrayed – Trusting, Loyal, Faithful
Abandoned – Included, Loved, Accepted, Recognized
Heartbroken – Healed, Whole, Joyful
Fearful – Brave, Courageous, Trusting, Confident, Secure
Grieving – Whole, Joyful, Peaceful, Thankful
Anxious – Confident, Relaxed, Calm, Composed
Depressed – Hopeful, Content, Cheerful, Happy
Bitter – Sweet, Generous, Forgiving, Grateful
Overwhelmed – Capable, Composed, Balanced
Frustrated – Patient, Content, Satisfied
Resentful – Forgiving, Accepting, Generous
Jealous – Content, Grateful, Trusting
Disappointed – Satisfied, Content, Pleased
Regretful – Accepting, At Peace, Learning
Guilty – Forgiven, Absolved, Innocent, Free
Hurt – Healed, Whole, Nurtured
Ashamed – Proud, Confident, Worthy
Lonely – Connected, Loved, Included

And if you can't remember the specific opposite to counter a negative emotion, just remember this: *love* is the positive opposite of all negative emotions. Love yourself enough to love without needing a specific reason, then loving all of life becomes easier. **Bask in love as if it were the very air around you, because it is.**